Mind Webs

LIVING THINGS

Anna Claybourne

Illustrated by Chrissy Barnard

First published in Great Britain in 2015 by Wayland

Dewey number: 570-dc23
ISBN: 978 0 7502 8960 3
Library Ebook ISBN: 978 0 7502 8791 3
10 9 8 7 6 5 4 3 2 1

MIX
Paper from
responsible sources
FSC® C104740
FSC
www.fsc.org

Series editor: Victoria Brooker
Series designer: Lisa Peacock

A CIP catalogue record for this book is available
from the British Library.

Wayland is an imprint of Hachette Children's Group
Part of Hodder & Stoughton
Carmelite House
50 Victoria Embankment
London EC4Y 0DZ

Printed in China

An Hachette UK Company
www.hachette.co.uk
www.hachettechildrens.co.uk

Contents

What are living things?

Our planet, the Earth, is the only planet we know of that is home to living things. Living things include plants, such as trees, grass and flowers, and animals, such as fish, frogs, birds, snakes, bees and elephants. Humans are a type of animal too.

There are also lots of fungi, including mushrooms and moulds, and micro-organisms – tiny living things too small for us to see. In fact, there are more micro-organisms than anything else. They include microscopic creatures living in seawater and in the soil, and tiny germs that cause diseases.

Species

Scientists have discovered and named around 1.5 million different types, or species, of living things. But there are many more still to be discovered. Scientists think there are probably more like 8 million species in total!

Each species can reproduce or have babies, making more living things like itself. In this way, a species can carry on existing through time. Living things have some other features in common too. As well as reproducing, they all move, grow, sense their surroundings, take in food, and turn food into energy they can use.

What is a mind web?

In this book, all the facts you need to know about living things are arranged into handy mind webs. A mind web is a way of laying out information about a topic on a single page. The topic title goes in the middle, with all the important facts and words arranged around it. There are lines to link things together, and little pictures to help you remember things.

Mind webs are great for helping you sort out, learn and remember facts and ideas. You can see a whole topic at a glance, and remind yourself all about it quickly and easily. Because the mind web looks like a picture, your brain may also find it easier to remember. Mind webs can also be called mind maps, spidergrams or spider graphs.

This mini mind web shows some of the main topics to do with living things.

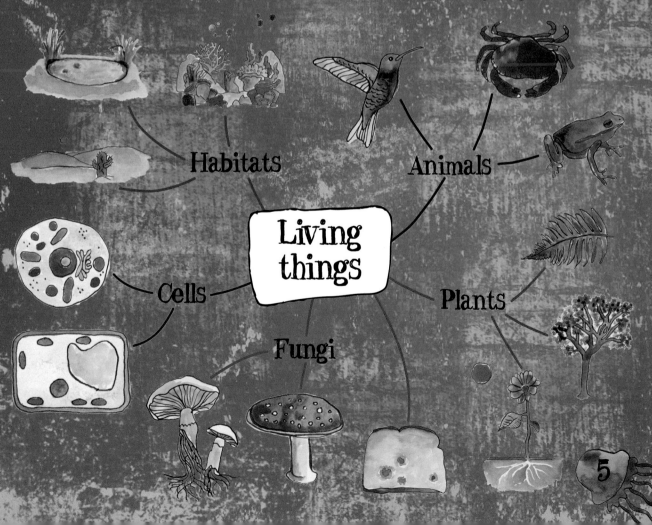

Habitats

Animals

Living things

Cells

Plants

Fungi

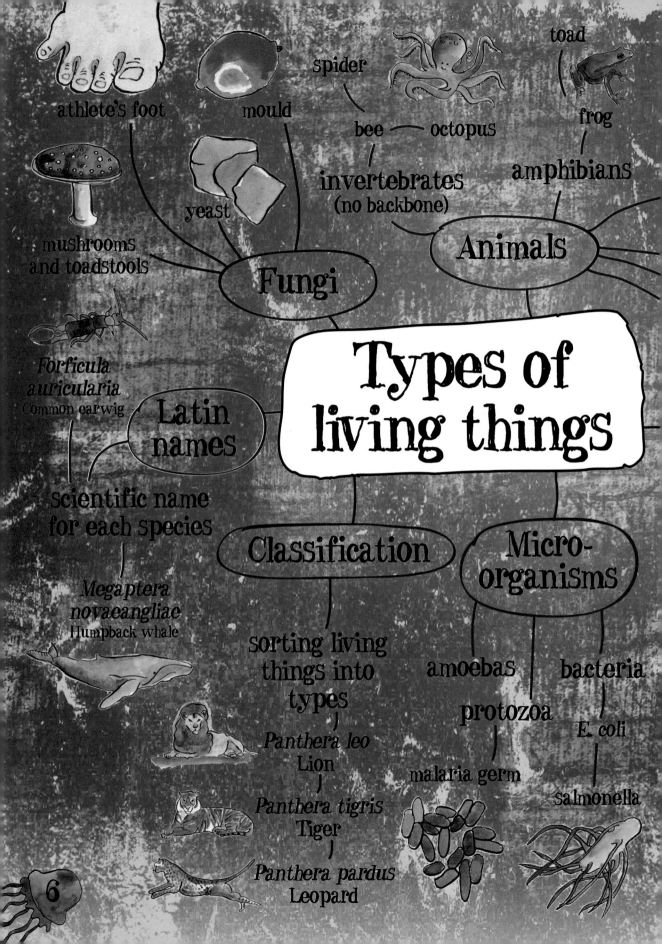

Types of living things

athlete's foot

mould

spider

bee — octopus

toad

frog

invertebrates
(no backbone)

amphibians

yeast

Animals

mushrooms
and toadstools

Fungi

*Forficula
auricularia*
Common earwig

**Latin
names**

scientific name
for each species

Classification

**Micro-
organisms**

*Megaptera
novaeangliae*
Humpback whale

sorting living
things into
types

amoebas

bacteria

protozoa

Panthera leo
Lion

malaria germ

E. coli

Panthera tigris
Tiger

salmonella

Panthera pardus
Leopard

6

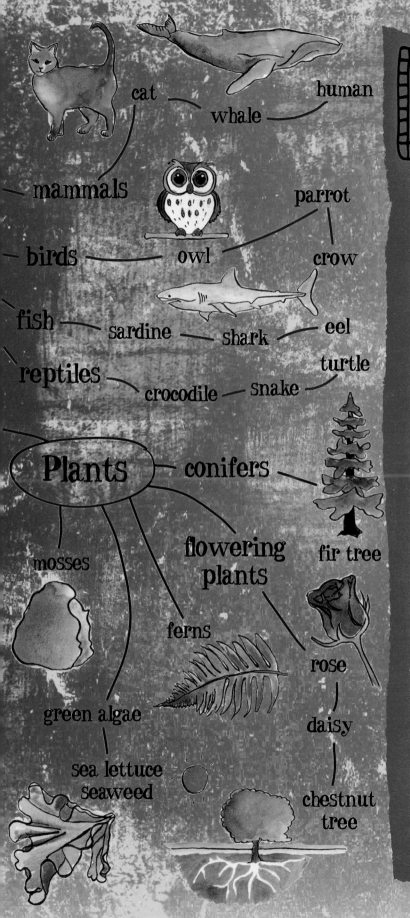

cat

whale

human

mammals

parrot

owl

crow

birds

owl

fish

sardine

shark

eel

turtle

reptiles

crocodile

snake

Plants

conifers

mosses

flowering plants

fir tree

ferns

green algae

rose

sea lettuce
seaweed

daisy

chestnut
tree

Scientists sort out living things into groups. This is called 'classification'. There are various ways of classifying living things, but they usually have the same main groups. They are:

Animals: Animals feed on other living things. They can usually move around on their own and react quickly to things around them.

Plants: Plants use light energy, usually from the Sun, to help them make food. They are usually green, have roots and stay in one place.

Fungi: Fungi are like plants, but they do not use sunlight to grow.

Other living things: The remaining living things are mainly microscopically small creatures, or micro-organisms. This group includes bacteria and other tiny creatures like amoebas.

Latin names
Each species of living thing also has its own scientific name, written in Latin.

Cells

All living things are made up of tiny units called cells. Most cells are so small, you can see them only with a microscope. That means a large living thing like a human being, an elephant or a tree is made up of millions and millions of cells. However, there are also many kinds of much smaller living things with far fewer cells. There are a huge number of singled-celled creatures – living things made up of just one cell.

What's in a cell?
A cell is a tiny unit. It has its own skin, called the cell membrane, and tiny working parts called organelles. The organelles do different jobs inside the cell, just as the organs in your body, like your heart, stomach and lungs, do different jobs in your body.

Types of cells
Cells vary depending on the job they do. A human has about 200 different types, such as brain, muscle, skin and blood cells. Animal cells, plant cells and single-celled bacteria are different from each other too.

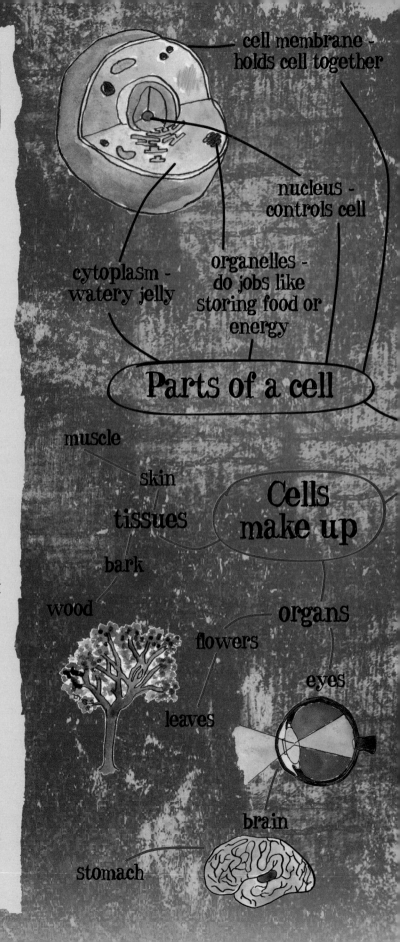

cell membrane - holds cell together

nucleus - controls cell

cytoplasm - watery jelly

organelles - do jobs like storing food or energy

Parts of a cell

muscle

skin

tissues

bark

wood

Cells make up

organs

flowers

eyes

leaves

brain

stomach

human -
about 10 trillion cells

elephant -
about 7,000
trillion cells

tiny worm -
about 1,000 cells

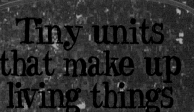
Tiny units
that make up
living things

bacteria -
1 cell each

Cells

Bacterial
cell

no separate
nucleus

tail-shaped
parts

organelles

cell wall

cell
membrane

Animal
cell

Plant
cell

nucleus

thick
cytoplasm

cell
membrane

large vacuole
or space

nucleus

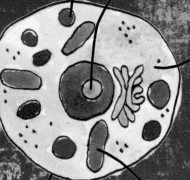

cell
membrane

organelles

organelles that
collect sunlight

strong outer
cell wall

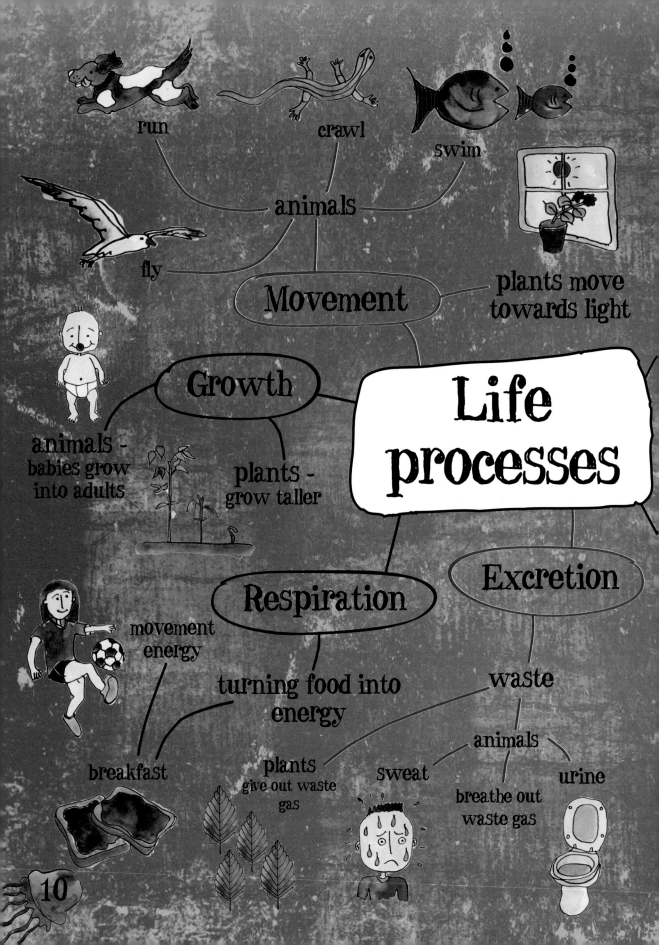

run

crawl

swim

animals

fly

Movement

plants move towards light

Growth

Life processes

animals - babies grow into adults

plants - grow taller

Excretion

Respiration

movement energy

turning food into energy

waste

breakfast

plants give out waste gas

sweat

animals

urine

breathe out waste gas

10

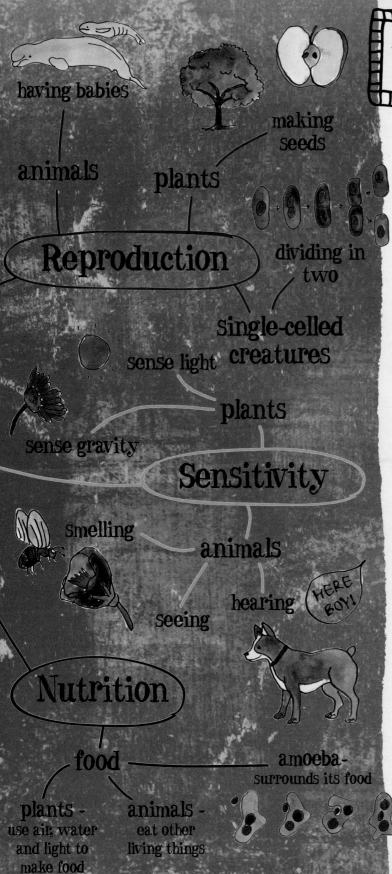

having babies

making seeds

animals

plants

Reproduction

dividing in two

single-celled creatures

sense light

plants

sense gravity

Sensitivity

smelling

animals

seeing

hearing

HERE BOY!

Nutrition

food

amoeba - surrounds its food

plants - use air, water and light to make food

animals - eat other living things

There are some things that all living creatures do, known as the life processes. There are seven main life processes:

Movement: All living things move. A plant moves towards the light as it grows.

Reproduction: Living things have babies, or make more copies of themselves. Wolves have cubs, plants make seeds that become new plants, and bacteria make copies of themselves by dividing in two.

Sensitivity: Living things can sense their surroundings. A tree's roots sense gravity to help them grow downward.

Nutrition: All living things take in some kind of food to live on.

Excretion: All living things excrete, or give out waste.

Respiration: Respiration means turning food chemicals into energy.

Growth: All living things grow.

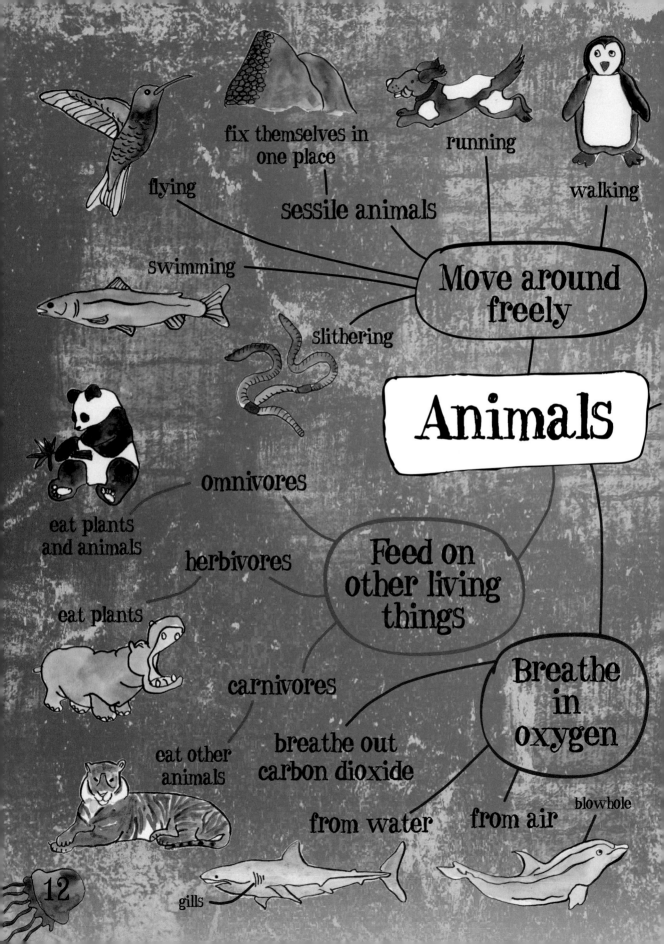

flying

fix themselves in
one place

running

walking

sessile animals

swimming

Move around
freely

slithering

Animals

omnivores

eat plants
and animals

herbivores

Feed on
other living
things

eat plants

carnivores

Breathe
in
oxygen

breathe out
carbon dioxide

eat other
animals

blowhole

from water

from air

12

gills

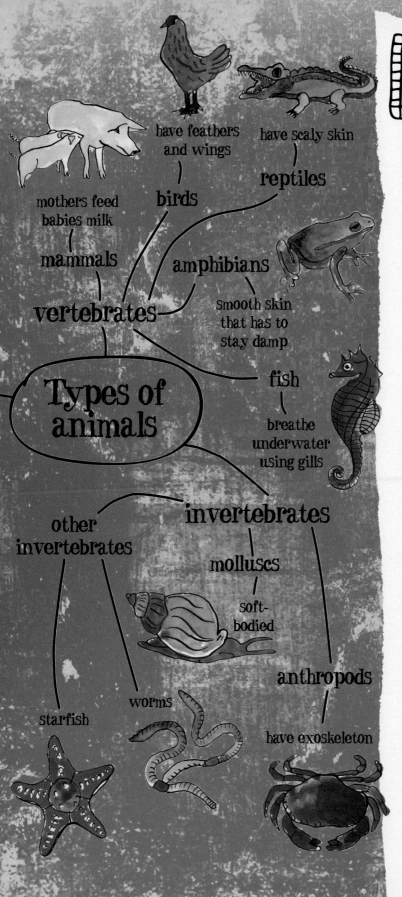

have feathers
and wings

have scaly skin

reptiles

birds

mothers feed
babies milk

mammals

amphibians

vertebrates

smooth skin
that has to
stay damp

**Types of
animals**

fish

breathe
underwater
using gills

invertebrates

other
invertebrates

molluscs

soft-
bodied

anthropods

worms

starfish

have exoskeleton

Animals

What are animals?
The main features of animals are that they feed on other living things, breathe in oxygen gas, and breathe out another gas, carbon dioxide (CO_2). The word 'animal' means something that breathes.

Most animals also move around freely and independently – meaning they can move by themselves and go where they like. A few of them, however, spend most of their lives staying still – such as mussels, which fix themselves to rocks.

Backbones or no backbones?
Scientists divide animals into two main groups – vertebrates (animals with backbones) and invertebrates, which have no backbone. Vertebrates, like humans, cats and birds, have not just a backbone, but a whole skeleton inside their bodies. Invertebrates, like slugs, spiders and snails, have a soft body, sometimes with a shell or a protective hard outer skin, or exoskeleton.

caterpillar

female
lays eggs

pupa inside
cocoon

male and
female cells

metamorphosis

two parents

adult

moth

Insects

cubs

male and
female cells

two
parents

mothers feed
baby milk

tiger

Mammals

growth
of bud

bud
develops
mouth and
tentacles

hydra

bud breaks
off

Budding

Reptiles

whiptail lizard

turtle

one parent

babies fend for
themselves

two parents

eggs
hatch

eggs

male and female
cells

gives birth
without mating

frogspawn

male and female cells

tadpoles

two parents

froglets

frog

Amphibians

Animal life cycles

Birds

chicken

two parents

chicks

male and female cells

eggs

Animals reproduce, or have babies, in several different ways. Most animals make babies by combining two cells – one from a male and one from a female. When they join, they make a new cell that can grow into a baby.

In many other animals, the parents mate, and the male and female cells join inside the female's body. The female may then lay eggs, or grow the babies inside her body, then give birth to them.

One parent
Some animals need only one parent to reproduce. For example, some species of lizards are all female, and have babies without mating. The hydra, a simple sea animal, can have babies by 'budding' – a small part of the parent grows into a baby, then breaks off.

Plants

Plants are found all over our planet, and some are among the biggest of all living things. Unlike animals, most plants are rooted into the soil, and do not move around much. When they do, they move slowly. Plants can sense light and gravity, but they don't have eyes, ears or mouths.

Green machines

Inside their cells, plants contain a green chemical called chlorophyll. Chlorophyll allows plants to make food by combining water and carbon dioxide gas (CO_2) from the air, using energy from the Sun. This process is called photosynthesis, and it happens inside a plant's leaves. Plants are mainly green because of the chlorophyll they contain.

Flowers or no flowers?

Most of the plants around us are flowering plants – like fruit trees, buttercups, garden roses and daffodils. However, conifers have cones instead of flowers, and there are some non-flowering plants such as ferns and mosses.

giant
sequoia
tree

up to 85
metres high

7.7 metres
across

Biggest plant

Plants

twigs

branches

trunk

Stems

trees

carry water around plant

wood

heartwood

tree rings

sapwood

outerwood

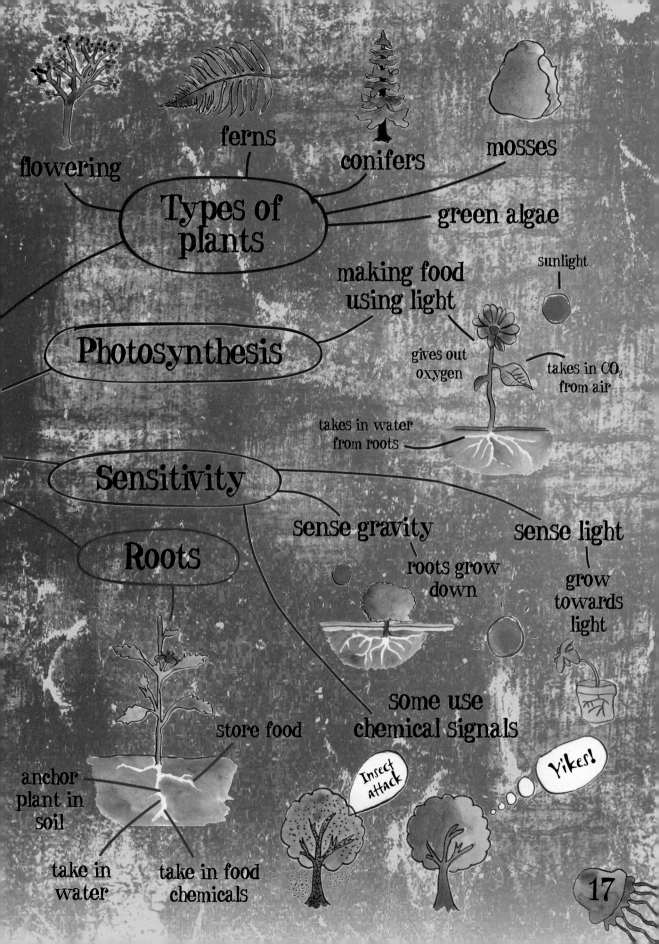

ferns

flowering

conifers

mosses

Types of plants

green algae

making food using light

sunlight

Photosynthesis

gives out oxygen

takes in CO_2 from air

takes in water from roots

Sensitivity

sense gravity

sense light

Roots

roots grow down

grow towards light

some use chemical signals

store food

anchor plant in soil

Insect attack

Yikes!

take in water

take in food chemicals

mosses

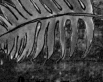

ferns

horsetails

release tiny spores
instead of a seed

apple tree

Seedless
plants

Plant life cycles

strawberry

stalks spread
sideways

runners

Spreading
out

rhizomes

Seed dispersal

roots spread
sideways

explodes to
shoot seeds

in animal
droppings

nettles

carried/
stored by
animals

squirting
cucumber

berries

chestnuts

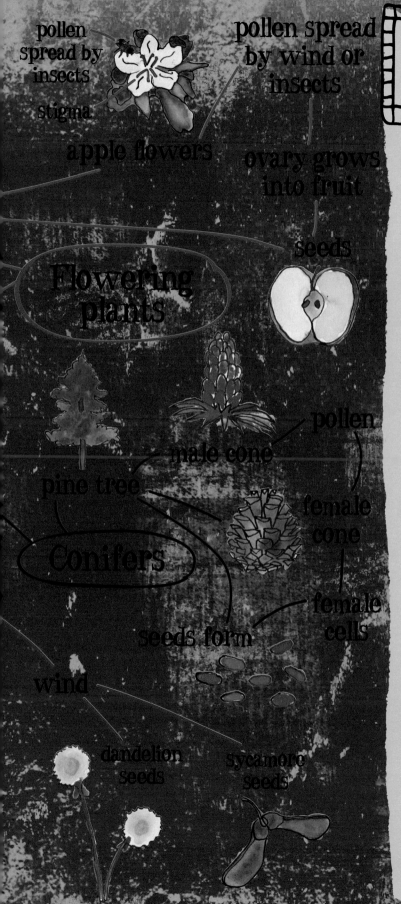

pollen spread by insects

stigma

apple flowers

pollen spread by wind or insects

ovary grows into fruit

seeds

Flowering plants

pollen

male cone

pine tree

female cone

Conifers

female cells

seeds form

wind

dandelion seeds

sycamore seeds

Plant life cycles

All plants reproduce and make baby plants like themselves. Like animals, they often do this by combining a male cell with a female cell. This makes a seed that can grow into a new plant. However, the male and female cells don't always come from different plants. Often they are both found on one plant.

Plants reproduce in other ways too. Some, like the dandelion, can make seeds without combining male and female cells. Others reach out sideways with special roots, called rhizomes, or stems, called runners. They grow into new plants that will separate from the parent plant.

Eat me!
Plant seeds often form inside sweet-tasting fruits like apples or cherries. Or the seed itself – like a chestnut – is delicious. Animals collect these, then drop them somewhere else, or eat them and spread the seeds around in their droppings. This helps the plant disperse its seeds far and wide.

19

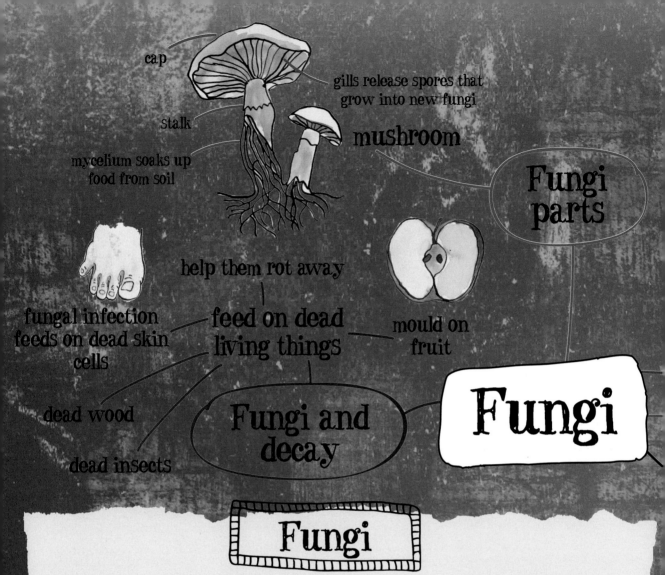

cap

gills release spores that
grow into new fungi

stalk

mushroom

mycelium soaks up
food from soil

Fungi
parts

help them rot away

fungal infection
feeds on dead skin
cells

feed on dead
living things

mould on
fruit

dead wood

Fungi and
decay

Fungi

dead insects

Fungi

Fungi are plant-like in some ways – they can grow in soil, and often have a network of thin, thread-like roots called the mycelium. But unlike plants, fungi are not green, and don't use sunlight to make food and grow. Instead, they feed on whatever they are growing on or in. Mushrooms often grow in soil or on old, dead wood. When you see mould growing on fruit or stale bread, that's a type of fungi too. Some fungi even grow on other living things, such as living plants, insects or even human skin.

How many cells?

Most types of fungi, like mushrooms and mould, have many cells. But one type, yeasts, are single-celled. They live together in big groups or colonies, so when you see fresh yeast, it looks a bit like a block of cheese. Yeast cells multiply, or increase in number, by budding. Each cell grows a new cell on its side, which gets bigger and bigger until it breaks off.

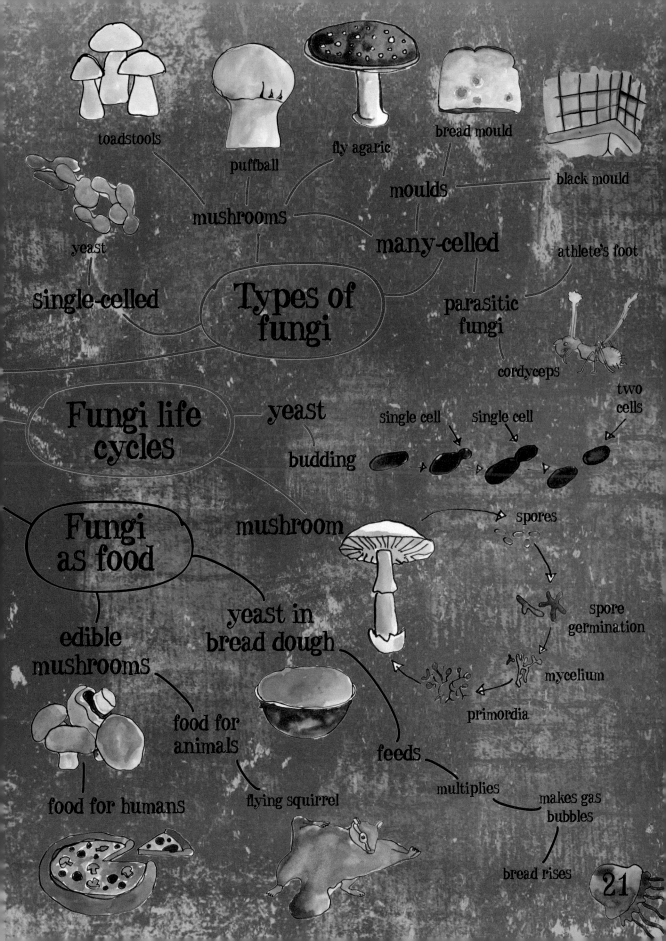

toadstools

fly agaric

puffball

bread mould

black mould

moulds

mushrooms

yeast

many-celled

single-celled

athlete's foot

Types of fungi

parasitic fungi

cordyceps

two cells

Fungi life cycles

yeast

single cell

single cell

budding

spores

mushroom

spore germination

Fungi as food

mycelium

yeast in bread dough

primordia

edible mushrooms

food for animals

feeds

food for humans

flying squirrel

multiplies

makes gas bubbles

bread rises

not fully 'living'

even smaller than bacteria

tardigrades

nematodes

copepods

measles

dust mites

tiny animals

chicken pox

flu

tiny fungi

yeast

survive by invading cells

cause diseases

green algae — tiny plants

tuberculosis

sleeping sickness

malaria

Viruses

whooping cough

protozoa

salmonella poisoning

bacteria —

Harmful micro-organisms

make yogurt

Helpful micro-organisms

protozoa

treat sewage

in plankton

bacteria

yeast

help digest food

making beer and wine

make soil fertile

making bread

provide food for sea creatures

make useful chemicals

22

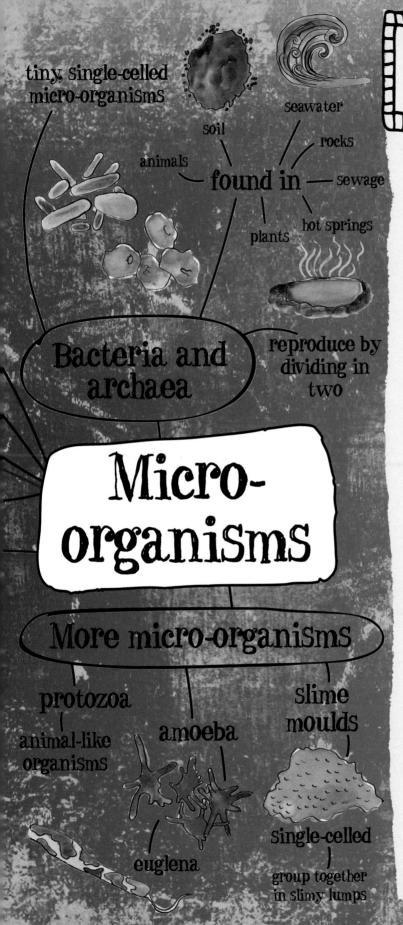

tiny, single-celled micro-organisms

soil

seawater

rocks

animals

found in — sewage

hot springs

plants

Bacteria and archaea

reproduce by dividing in two

Micro-organisms

More micro-organisms

protozoa

amoeba

slime moulds

animal-like organisms

euglena

single-celled

group together in slimy lumps

Micro-organisms are living things that are so small, we have to look at them with a microscope.

Types of micro-organisms
Scientists have discovered a **LOT** of different species of micro-organisms. Because they are so hard to see, there are probably many more still waiting to be found. Micro-organisms include the smallest members of the animal, plant and fungi families. They also include bacteria, and their relatives the archaea. These tiny creatures exist in huge numbers in all kinds of places – in soil, in water, deep in underground rocks, and inside larger living things, including humans. A large handful of soil contains more bacteria than there are human beings on Earth.

Helpful and harmful
Some micro-organisms are harmful to humans and can invade our bodies, causing diseases like tuberculosis and malaria. But others are helpful – for example, the bacteria living in our intestines help us to digest food.

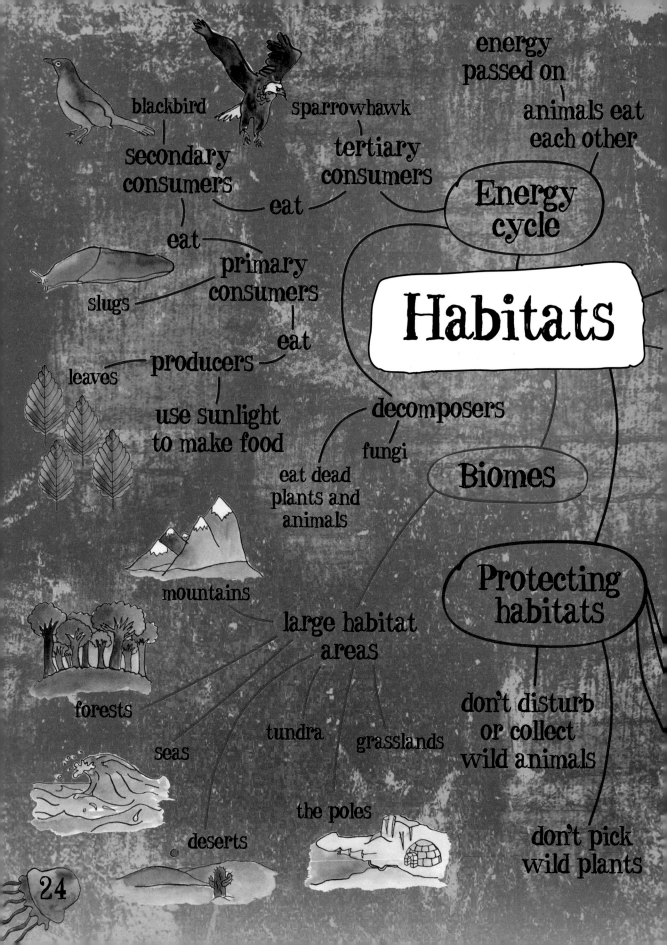

blackbird

sparrowhawk

secondary consumers

tertiary consumers

energy passed on

animals eat each other

Energy cycle

eat

eat

primary consumers

slugs

eat

Habitats

producers

leaves

decomposers

use sunlight to make food

fungi

eat dead plants and animals

Biomes

mountains

Protecting habitats

large habitat areas

forests

don't disturb or collect wild animals

seas

tundra

grasslands

the poles

deserts

don't pick wild plants

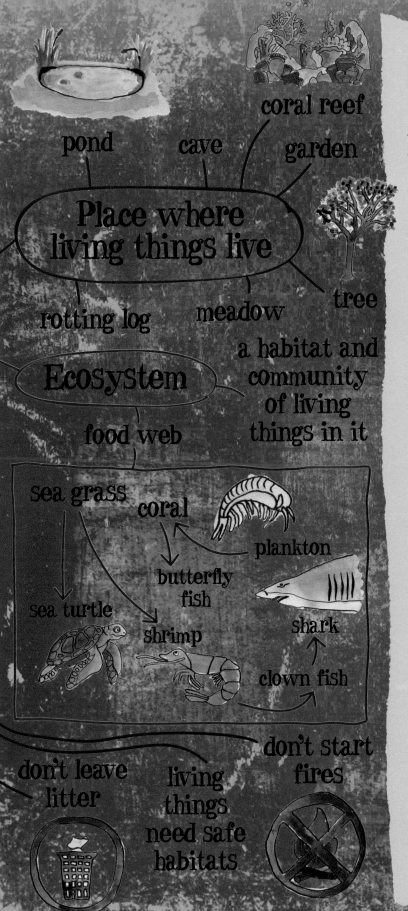

coral reef

pond   cave   garden

Place where living things live

rotting log   meadow   tree

Ecosystem

a habitat and community of living things in it

food web

sea grass

coral

plankton

butterfly fish

sea turtle

shrimp

shark

clown fish

don't start fires

don't leave litter   living things need safe habitats

A habitat is the place where a species lives. All living things have their own habitats, where they can survive and find food. For example, a koala's habitat is a eucalyptus tree. Koalas are good at climbing and hanging onto branches, and they feed on eucalyptus leaves. If a koala didn't have this habitat to live in, it would be hard for it to survive.

Habitats can be quite small — a tree, pond, cave or garden could be a habitat. Biomes are larger areas that have a particular type of climate and surroundings — such as forests, deserts and mountain ranges.

Living together
Together, a habitat and the living things that live in it are called an ecosystem. In an ecosystem, each creature survives by feeding on something else that lives there. These relationships can be shown as food chains. A network of the food chains found in one ecosystem is called a food web.

Adaptation

Living things are amazingly well-suited to the places they live in. A whale, for example, has a streamlined shape for moving through water, thick blubber to keep it warm and a blowhole to help them breathe. All these features help it to survive in the ocean. But if you took a whale to live in the rainforest, it wouldn't last long!

Adapting to fit

Living things gradually adapt, or change over time, to suit their habitats. All species have variation. This means that they vary, or have slight differences from each other – even within the same species. In each habitat, the living things that survive best are the ones that suit that habitat best. They will find more food, escape from predators better and live longer. This means they are more likely to have babies and keep the species alive.

Living things pass on their features to their babies. So the features that suit the habitat best get passed on. Over time, species change, becoming adapted to their habitats. Another name for this is evolution.

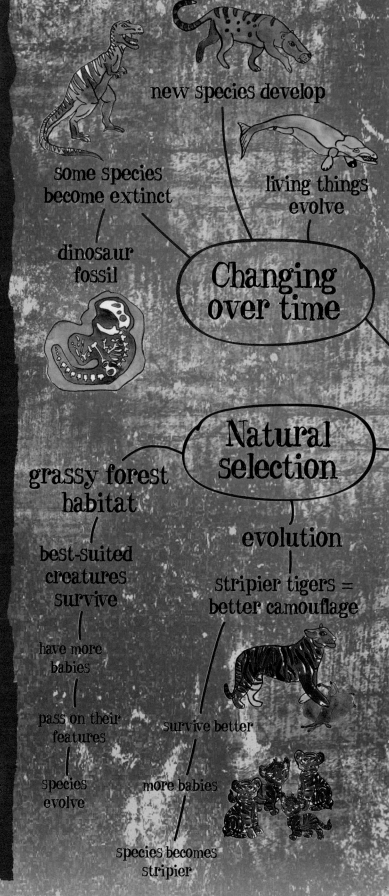

new species develop

some species become extinct

living things evolve

dinosaur fossil

Changing over time

Natural selection

grassy forest habitat

best-suited creatures survive

have more babies

pass on their features

species evolve

evolution

stripier tigers = better camouflage

survive better

more babies

species becomes stripier

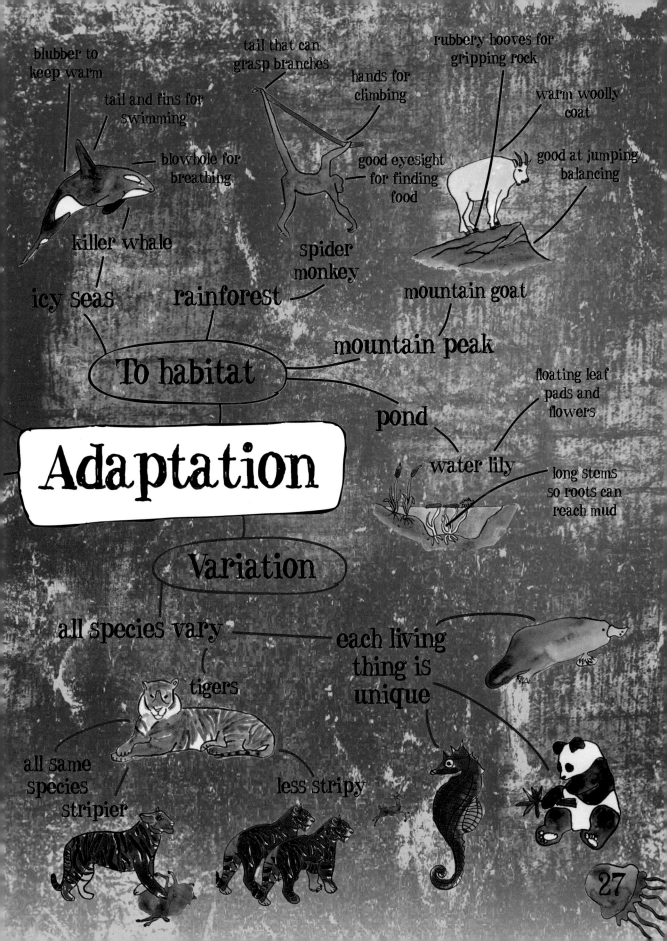

blubber to
keep warm

tail and fins for
swimming

blowhole for
breathing

killer whale

icy seas

tail that can
grasp branches

hands for
climbing

good eyesight
for finding
food

spider
monkey

rainforest

rubbery hooves for
gripping rock

warm woolly
coat

good at jumping/
balancing

mountain goat

mountain peak

To habitat

Adaptation

pond

floating leaf
pads and
flowers

water lily

long stems
so roots can
reach mud

Variation

all species vary

each living
thing is
unique

tigers

all same
species
stripier

less stripy

Genes and DNA

All living things have DNA in their cells. DNA (short for DeoxyriboNucleic Acid) is a chemical that forms long, thin strings. They are found coiled up inside cells. Genes are sections of DNA. Each gene contains instructions in a code that cells can read and understand. The instructions tell cells how to work and what to do.

Building a body
Each species has its own genome, or set of genes, which decide how it grows and what it looks like. For example, tigers' genes give them

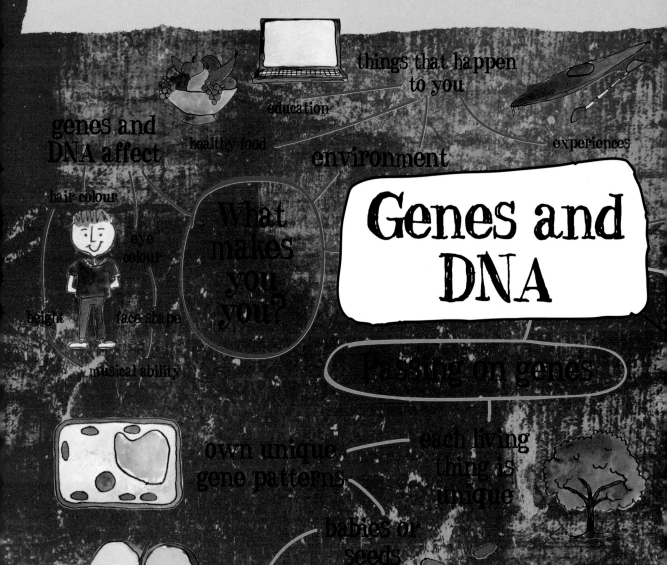

things that happen to you

education

genes and DNA affect

healthy food

environment

experiences

hair colour

eye colour

What makes you you?

Genes and DNA

height   face shape

musical ability

Passing on genes

own unique gene patterns

each living thing is unique

babies or seeds

genes got passed on

28

their big, strong bodies, stripy fur and sharp claws. Daisies have a different set of genes that make them grow roots, a stem and white flowers.

Genes also vary slightly within species. That's why daisies are slightly different from each other. So are people. Your genes make you a human, like other humans – but they also make you an individual, not quite like anyone else.

Passing it on
Whenever living things reproduce, they pass on copies of their genes to their babies. That's why tigers have baby tigers and daisy seeds grow into new daisies. It also explains why features like musical ability or red hair run in families.

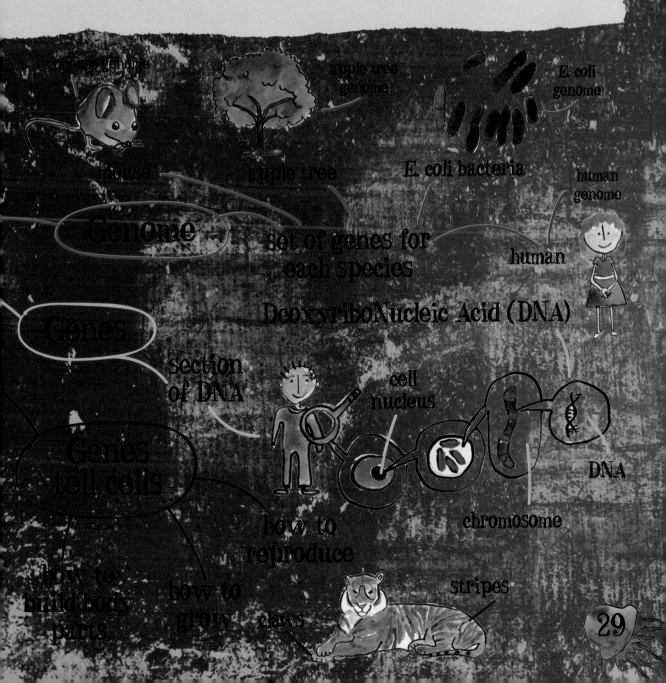

mouse genome

apple tree genome

E. coli genome

mouse

apple tree

E. coli bacteria

human genome

human

Genome

set of genes for each species

DeoxyriboNucleic Acid (DNA)

Genes

section of DNA

cell nucleus

DNA

Genes tell cells

chromosome

how to reproduce

how to build body parts

how to grow

claws

stripes

Glossary

adaptation Changing to become more suited to the environment.

amoeba A type of single-celled living thing.

animal Living thing that breathes, moves around and eats other living things.

archaea A type of tiny single-celled living thing.

bacteria A type of tiny single-celled living thing.

biome Large area of a particular type of habitat.

blowhole Breathing hole on the head of a whale or dolphin.

blubber Thick layer of fat under the skin.

budding Way of reproducing in which the parent grows a baby from part of its body, which then breaks off.

carbon dioxide Gas found in the air, excreted by animals and taken in by plants.

cells Tiny units that make up all living things.

cell membrane Outer skin surrounding a cell.

chlorophyll Green chemical found in plant cells and used to collect sunlight.

classification The sorting of living things into groups and types.

DNA (DeoxyriboNucleic Acid) Spiral strand-shaped chemical that genes are made of.

disperse Spread out over a wide area.

ecosystem A habitat and the living things that are found in it.

evolution The way species change over time to become better at surviving.

excretion Giving out waste products, one of the life processes.

exoskeleton Hard outer skin or shell found on some invertebrates.

food chain Sequence of living things in which each one is food for the next.

food web Network of the various food chains that make up an ecosystem.

fungi Type of living thing that includes mushrooms, moulds and yeast.

genes Instructions found in cells that tell living things how to live and grow.

genome Set of genes belonging to a particular species.

habitat Place or surroundings where a living things live.

invertebrate Animal without a backbone.

larva Name for the young of some types of insects and other animals.

life processes Things that all living things do as part of being alive.

metamorphosis Changing shape or form as part of the life cycle of a living thing.

micro-organism Tiny living thing that is too small to be seen without a microscope.

mycelium Network of thread-like roots or hairs found in many fungi.

nucleus Control centre of a cell.

nutrition Another name for food and feeding, and one of the life processes.

organelles Tiny mini-organs found inside cells.

oxygen Gas found in the air, excreted by plants and taken in by animals.

photosynthesis Making food using carbon dioxide, water and sunlight.

plant Living thing that uses sunlight to make food and is usually rooted in one place.

predator Animal that hunts and eats other animals.

primordia An organ or part in the earliest stage of development.

reproduce To have babies or young.

respiration Converting food into useful energy, one of the life processes.

rhizome Plant root that grows sideways underground and gives rise to new plants.

runner Plant stem that grows sideways and roots into the soil to create new plants.

sensitivity Ability to sense and respond to surroundings, and one of the life processes.

single-celled Having only one cell.

species A particular type of living thing.

variation Slight differences between living things, including within the same species.

vertebrate Animal with a backbone.

yeast Type of single-celled fungus.

Index